The Prophetic Almanac 2025

By
Pastor Bill Jenkins

Table of Contents

Introduction

Another year, another prophetic almanac. The question always is, "What will this specific year hold for the child of God?" This is definitely going to be a year when America will reap what it has sown.

Galatians 6:7, "Do not be deceived: God cannot be mocked. A man reaps what he sows".

Our choices have been made and our voices have been heard. Now is the time for us to get what we think we want by casting our votes and making our decisions. The rewards or consequences of our actions at this present moment will shape our future and determine the quality of our lives moving forward.

Sow a Thought, Reap a Habit

Sow a Habit, Reap a Character

Sow a Character, Reap a Destiny

Our destiny is determined by our actions and by our decisions. Although that may sound a little scary, do not fear because…

GOD IS STILL IN CONTROL!!

"In him we were also chosen,[a] having been predestined according to the plan of him who works out everything in conformity with the purpose of his will," Ephesians 1:11 (NIV)

"For dominion belongs to the Lord and he rules over the nations." Psalm 22:28, (NIV)

"Many are the plans in a person's heart, but it is the Lord's purpose that prevails."
Proverbs 19:21 (NIV)

"But if it is from God, you will not be able to stop these men; you will only find yourselves fighting against God." Acts 5:39 (NIV)

"Why, you do not even know what will happen tomorrow. What is your life? You are a mist that appears for a little while and then vanishes. Instead, you ought to say, 'If it is the Lord's will, we will live and do this or that." James 4:14-15 (NIV)

God's Will Cannot Be Stopped
by Man's Decisions

God has not given us a spirit of fear. God has given us a sound mind when we lean on and learn from God's Word. Above all, this is a Year of Grace. 25 is made by multiplying 5x5. When the number five is mentioned in the Bible, it revolves around grace.

- The Tabernacle was measured in multiples of five.

- In the Old Covenant, five types of animals were sacrificed: goats, sheep, cattle, pigeons, and doves.

- There were five main wounds Jesus suffered on the cross.

- There were five wise and unwise virgins used in the parable of Jesus in Matthew 25.

So, if it takes 5x5 to get to 25, this is not only a year of grace, it is a year of GRACE QUINTUPLED.

God is giving us His grace, or His unmerited favor, to deal with and handle anything that comes our way in 2025!!! There will be ups and downs, roadblocks and obstacles, successes and failures, but God will bring us through them all. God does not always take us out of the fire, but He never leaves us alone. If He does not remove us from the storm, He will show up in the middle of the storm. Get ready for an interesting year with a lot of unpredictable events happening all around us. It is a one-of-a-kind year. Just as God gave Paul the grace to deal with his thorn in the flesh, God will give you the grace, or the God-given ability, to deal with all your troubles. You will not just make it; you will come out on top. Victory is yours because God's grace is yours in 2025!!

Chapter 1
Preview

Previews are much like movie trailers. They do not give you all the details of what is to come, but they give you enough of an overview of what is to come. In this chapter, I give you some things and people to be looking out for in 2025. All these things are designed to help you become more spiritually sensitive. Look for these things in the news and other media and connect them to the vision of 2025.

Sport of the Year
Volleyball

State of the Year
Arkansas
The 25th state to join the Union on June 15, 1836

City of the Year
Las Vegas, Nevada

Planet of the Year
Saturn

Bible Characters of the Year
Men – Philemon
Women – Abigail
Youth – Jude

Bible Story of the Year
Jesus walking on the water
Matthew 14:22-33; Mark 6:45-52; John 6:16-21

Scripture of the Year
"As cold waters to a thirsty soul, so is good news from a far country." Proverbs 25:25

Book of the Bible of the Year
Ezekiel

Fruit of the Spirit of the Year
Patience

Gift of the Spirit for the Year
Word of Wisdom

Word of the Year
Grace

Color of the Year
Silver

Super Food of the Year
Grapes

Vegetable of the Year
Zucchini

Snack of the Year
Yogurt

Geographical Places of the Year

- Mediterranean Sea
- Nicaragua
- Iran
- Israel
- United States
- Italy
- China
- Ukraine

Animal of the Year
Snakes

I am going with snakes as the animal of the year, and I am not picking a specific snake on purpose. In my opinion, I have never met a good snake. Even in China, it is the year of the snake. But spiritually speaking, it is a year Christians must be aware of snakes. Snakes are symbols of Satan and his effort to deceive God's people. Snakes are mentioned around fifty times in the Bible, and they represent evil and deception. The first mention of Satan in the Bible came in Genesis 3 where he was called a serpent who tempted Adam and Eve to eat the forbidden fruit. Jesus and John the Baptist condemned the Pharisees by calling them a "brood of vipers" or "snakes." Paul was bitten by a snake, but God's healing power came upon him to undo the intended curse of the poisonous snake. Snakes are the first animal mentioned in the Bible which makes them the oldest animal in our universe. Snakes always have and always will be connected to Satan. So, beware of all the enemy's tactics in 2025.

Characteristics of a Snake

Positive	Negative
- Smart	- Stubborn
- Fast	- Overconfident
- Good Eyesight	- Territorial
- Determined	- Eat Dirt

- Hard Workers
- Calm
- Passionate
- Good Memories
- Resourceful
- Discerning
- Strong
- Adapt Easily

- Sharp Teeth
- Venomous
- Change Their Skin
- Suspicious
- Secretive
- Easily Provoked
- Like Darkness
- Isolation

Prophetic Dates of the Year

1. Saturday, January 25, 2025
2. Tuesday, February 25, 2025
3. Tuesday, March 25, 2025
4. Friday, April 25, 2025
5. Sunday, May 25, 2025
6. Wednesday, June 25, 2025
7. Friday, July 25, 2025
8. Monday, August 25, 2025
9. Thursday, September 25, 2025
10. Saturday, October 25, 2025
11. Tuesday, November 25, 2025
12. Thursday, December 25, 2025

25 Movies of the Year

1. In the Grey
2. Captain America: Brave New World
3. Thunderbolts
4. Mission Impossible 8
5. F1
6. Superman
7. Sinners
8. Disney's Snow White
9. AI to Knights
10. A Minecraft Movie
11. Michael
12. Jurassic Park Rebirth
13. The Fantastic Four: First Steps
14. Animal Friends
15. The Bride
16. Now You See Me 3
17. The Running Man
18. Wicked: Part Two
19. Dirty Dancing 2
20. Mortal Kombat 2
21. Predator: Badlands
22. Elio
23. Karate Kid: Legends
24. Sponge Bob Movie: Search for Squarefoot
25. Avatar: Fire and Ash

25 People to Watch in 2025

1. Donald Trump, President
2. Adele, Singer
3. Travis Hunter, Football Player
4. Sean Combs AKA P. Diddy, Rapper
5. Blake Lively, Actress
6. Kylian Mbappe, Soccer Player
7. J.D. Vance, Vice President
8. Patrick Mahomes, Football Player
9. Anthony Mackie, Actor
10. Volodymyr Zelenskyy, Ukraine President
11. Kendrick Lamar, Rapper
12. Harrison Ford, Actor
13. Elon Musk, Entrepreneur
14. John Thune, Senator Majority Leader
15. Ric Flair, Wrestler
16. Cooper Flagg, Basketball Player
17. Alicia Keys, Singer
18. Mike Myers, Actor
19. Mike Lee, Politician
20. Eminem, Rapper
21. Will Smith, Actor
22. Paige Bueckers, Basketball Player
23. Claudia Sheinbaum, President of Mexico
24. Jamie Dimon, Financial Executive
25. Robert Kennedy Jr., Politician

Chapter 2
Fun Facts About 2025

General

- 25 degrees Celsius is equal to 77 degrees Fahrenheit.
- The 25th year of marriage is known as the "Silver Anniversary," and silver is the recognized gift to commemorate the anniversary.
- In Great Britain, the slang term "pony" refers to £25.
- In Ireland, there is a card game known as Twenty-Five.
- The national game of India "Pachisi" means twenty-five in Hindi.
- There are twenty-five cents in a quarter dollar.
- Twenty-five percent is equal to 1/4.
- The 25th letter of the English and Roman alphabet is Y.
- 2025 is MMXXV in Roman numerals.
- Manganese has an atomic number of twenty-five.
- In Portugal, the maximum life sentence is 25 years imprisonment.

Entertainment

- Adele made an album titled *25*.
- Chicago (The band) has a song titled "25 or 6 to 4."

- *25th Hour* is a 2002 American drama film directed by Spike Lee and stars Edward Norton.
- There is a game show called 25 Words or Less.
- "25 Minutes to Go" is a song by Johnny Cash.
- Eminem has a song called "25 to Life."

Biblical

- The number 25 is used 23 times in the Bible.
- Only 17 out of 66 books of the Bible have a 25th chapter.
- Both the New Testament books of Philemon and Jude have only one chapter, which is composed of 25 verses.
- In the Bible, the book of 2 Kings contains 25 chapters.
- In the Old Testament, these Biblical chapters contain exactly 25 verses in the King James Bible:
  - Genesis 2
  - Exodus 2, 7, 19
  - Numbers 24
  - Deuteronomy 6, 23
  - Judges 7, 13, 21
  - 1 Samuel 12, 26, 28
  - 2 Samuel 5, 24
  - 2 Kings 2, 13
  - 2 Chronicles 33
  - Job 12, 24, 29
  - Proverbs 13

- Isaiah 7, 19, 22, 42, 45, 65
    - Jeremiah 3, 10
    - Ezekiel 11, 45
- In the New Testament, these chapters contain exactly 25 verses in the King James Bible:
    - Matthew 1, 4
    - John 2, 21
    - Acts 12
    - Romans 4, 7
    - Colossians 3
    - 1 Timothy 5
    - Hebrews 13
    - 1 Peter 1, 2
- According to Numbers 8:24, Levites were required to be at least twenty-five years old before they could begin their service at the temple. This age requirement emphasizes the importance of maturity and readiness for sacred duties. However, from the time of David onward, the minimum age was lowered to twenty, likely due to the increasing workload (1 Chronicles 23:24, Ezra 3:8).
- The number 25 plays a prominent role in Ezekiel's visions of the temple, which he saw in the twenty-fifth year of Judah's captivity (Ezekiel 40:1). There are at least five measurements within the prophetic temple that are twenty-five cubits long (40:13, 21, 25, 29 - 30).
- Ezekiel is shown, in a vision, 25 temple priests who are standing in the inner court of Jerusalem's temple. These men, with their backs to the temple,

are performing the abominable act of worshiping the sun as it rises in the east (Ezekiel 8:15 - 17).

- Ezekiel, in a later vision, is shown the eastern gate of Jerusalem's temple. He sees twenty-five princes, who were possibly civil magistrates, whom the Lord gives wicked advice and deceives the people into thinking the city is not in peril of being destroyed (Ezekiel 11:1 - 3).
- Ezekiel experienced his vision of the temple in the 25th year of his imprisonment.
- Words that are used 25 times in the Bible:
    - Occasion
    - Teaching
    - Willingly
    - Rebuked
- If you count the throne of God, there are twenty-five thrones mentioned in Revelation 4:4 (NIV). Surrounding the throne were twenty-four other thrones, and seated on them were twenty-four elders. Twenty-four plus one equals twenty-five.
- The 25th time Noah's name is mentioned marked the beginning of a new era of grace after the judgment and destruction of the Flood.
- Jotham was twenty-five years old when he became king and reigned sixteen years in Jerusalem. His mother's name was Jerushah, the daughter of Zadok (2 Chronicles 27:1).
- The construction of the Tabernacle in Exodus 25:1- 9, God gives Moses detailed instructions for building the Tabernacle, a sacred dwelling place for

His presence. The materials used in the construction, such as gold, silver, and bronze, carry significant spiritual meaning, highlighting the importance of purity, redemption, and judgment.

- Numbers 7 describes the dedication of the Tabernacle, which lasted for 12 days. During this time, the tribal leaders presented their offerings, totaling 25. This holy number signifies the completeness and fullness of their devotion to God.
- 25 is connected to Jesus walking on water. In John 6:19, Jesus walks 25 furlongs or over 3 miles on water to reach His disciples who are struggling in the middle of the Sea of Galilee.
- Hezekiah became king when he was twenty-five years old, and he reigned twenty-nine years in Jerusalem. His mother's name was Abijah, the daughter of Zechariah (2 Chronicles 29:1).
- King Jehoshaphat reigned for 25 years.

Sports
- In baseball, the number 25 jersey was worn by:
    - Mark McGwire
    - Barry Bonds
    - Jim Thome
    - Sammy Sosa
- In a Major League Baseball team, 25 was the size of a full roster team for most of the season.
- The first two sets in volleyball are played to 25 points and the third set to 15 points. Each set must

be won by two points. The first team to win two sets is the winner of the match.

History

- The 25th Amendment to the U.S. Constitution clarifies that the vice president becomes president if the president dies, resigns, or is removed from office by impeachment.
- William McKinley was the 25th President of the United States, serving from March 4, 1897, until his assassination on September 14, 1901. McKinley's presidency saw rapid economic growth.
- In 1947, scrolls were discovered in the Dead Sea region of Israel. Among all the scrolls found over the years, 25 copies of the Book of Deuteronomy have been identified.
- In the USA, twenty-five is the minimum age to serve in the US House of Representatives.

Chapter 3
2025 Vision

One of the most essential things we need to start a year and experience success in that year is to know the heart of God. Knowing the heart of God is knowing the will of God.

"And be not conformed to this world: but be ye transformed by the renewing of your mind, that ye may prove (discern) what is that good, and acceptable, and perfect, will of God." Romans 12:2 (KJV emphasis added)

There are approximately 31,102 verses in the Bible, and every one of them can send us a message from God to know His perfect will for our personal lives. If every verse is important, then every word is important. Some words are more descriptive and definitive than others, including scriptures with colors, names, places, people, symbols, and yes even … numbers. I am using the number 25 in this book as a map to help guide us to discover God's will for 2025. This is not magic or numerology; this is wisdom, and it pleases the Lord when we seek Him to understand His will.

"It is the glory of God to conceal a thing, but the honor of kings is to search out a matter." Proverbs 25:2

God sometimes hides things from us, so we will seek Him and develop our relationship with Him. Diligently seeking out truth from scripture helps us not rush to judgment or come to conclusions that may not be from God. The Bible commands us to "study," not just "read" the Word of God. Studying is about examining and analyzing to reach a conclusion. Too many times pastors release a vision for the New Year because they feel it is their duty, and although it may be good, it may not be exactly what God wants to say to His people. A vision for the year should be a vision for the year, not a vision for the first two weeks of the year. When I release a vision for the year, I am using the Word of God to accomplish that goal. This year, I am investing time to investigate the number 25 in scripture to give us answers in knowing God's perfect will for 2025. So… are you ready? Do you want God's vision for you in 2025?

Let me sum it up with five words:

GRACE, GRACE, GRACE, GRACE, and GRACE!!!

Yes, God's favor is on you in 2025 but wait … the number five in the Bible is connected to grace. So, if it takes 5x5 to get to 25, this is not only a Year of Grace it is a year of GRACE QUINTUPLED. Hallelujah!!!!! It is grace upon grace upon grace upon grace upon grace. It is favor upon favor upon favor upon favor upon favor.

Not only does this scripture prove Jesus is greater than Moses, but it also proves that even though the law was good, grace is better. God is the inventor and creator of grace. If it were not for God's grace, we would have already been eternally punished for our sins. God the Father sent His only Son to die on the cross for our sins, to be the only one to funnel grace from Heaven to Earth. Jesus' death provides the opportunity for us to not only be saved but to also experience God's grace when we sin after salvation. It also gives us the help we need to be successful in life and avoid the ultimate punishment of sin which is death. Grace is defined as the unmerited and undeserved favor of God. Grace is getting something good that you do not deserve and not getting something bad that you do deserve. It is also important to understand that although grace is one of God's greatest gifts to mankind, it is not a license to freely sin and be disobedient to God. It is not an unconditional covering that allows us to be forgiven of things we continually do without truly changing our lives. Grace is not a free pass to commit sin and stay the way you are in your life. The grace of God will change us from the inside out when we understand exactly what God's grace is all about.

Ten Facts About God's Grace

1. We are *Saved* by Grace.
   The only way to salvation is through the doorway of grace. We cannot earn it. We cannot work for it. We cannot buy it from Amazon.

   "For by grace are ye saved through faith; and that not of yourselves: it is the gift of God: Not of works, lest any man should boast." Ephesians 2:8-9

2. We are *Forgiven* by Grace.
   Though we do not deserve it, God wipes our sin slate clean by His grace.

   "I, even I, am he that blotteth out thy transgressions for mine own sake, and will not remember thy sins." Isaiah 43:25

3. We are *Healed* by Grace.
   God heals our broken hearts and our sick bodies. He binds up our wounds and our emotions even though we do not deserve it. God is our healer.

"He healeth the broken in heart, and bindeth up their wounds." Psalm 147:3

4. We are *Liberated* by Grace.

   Grace gives us the ability to be free from things that are holding us back from fulfilling our destiny.

   "If the Son therefore shall make you free, ye shall be free indeed." John 8:36

5. We are given *Talents* by Grace.

   God has gifted and given each of us the ability to do something well. We are to use those abilities to build the Kingdom of God.

   "As every man hath received the gift, even so minister the same one to another, as good stewards of the manifold grace of God." 1 Peter 4:10

6. We are *Kept* by Grace.

   We cannot just lose our salvation. It is a gift of God. If we could earn it, then we could lose it the moment we stopped earning it. God saves us and keeps us by His grace.

   "Now unto him that is able to keep you from falling, and to present you faultless before the presence of his glory with exceeding joy." Jude 1:24

7. We are *Transformed* by Grace.

Through His grace, God makes us new and changes us through the renewing of our minds.

"And be not conformed to this world: but be ye transformed by the renewing of your mind, that ye may prove what is that good, and acceptable, and perfect, will of God." Romans 12:2

8. We are able to *Forgive* others and ourselves by Grace.

Forgiving others and forgiving ourselves is essential to a healthy spiritual relationship with God. If we cannot do it on our own …. God's grace will help us. It is the power to do what we do not have the power to do.

God's Grace Is the Power to Do What We Do Not Have the Power to Do

---

"Forbearing one another, and forgiving one another, if any man have a quarrel against any: even as Christ forgave you, so also do ye." Colossians 3:13

9. We are able to remain *Humble* by Grace.

When pride causes us to drift away from the Lord, grace brings us back to the cross.

"But he giveth more grace. Wherefore he saith, God resisteth the proud, but giveth grace unto the humble." James 4:6

10. We are able to *Love* by Grace.
    True love only comes from above (God), so it takes grace to offer love to others.

"We love him, because he first loved us."
1 John 4:19

The word "grace" is the English translation of the Greek word "charis", which appears in the New Testament about 150 times. Grace is a gift from God that should be cherished by every Christian. Grace only comes from God.

Grace is …
- Unmerited Favor
- Spiritual Empowerment
- Forgiveness
- Love
- Acceptance
- Compassion
- Understanding
- Divine Influence
- Freedom
- Transformation
- Godly Assistance
- Kindness

This is a year of GRACE QUINTUPLED. Do not look to just receive God's grace; look for opportunities to share God's grace with others. Look to receive and give grace five times more in 2025 than you ever have before. Trust me when I say, you will need God's grace more this year than you ever have needed it before. Learn to make grace a part of your daily life. Premeditate grace every morning you wake up, so you can practice grace when you deal with others. God's grace is sufficient for all your needs, wants, desires, and shortcomings in 2025!!!

Chapter 4
The Bible Speaks

GENESIS 25
The Power of Prayer

This is a busy chapter with a lot going on. Abraham marries Keturah and has at least six children with her. Abraham then left the majority of what he owned to Isaac before dying at 175 years of age. The illegitimate son of Abraham, Ishmael, then dies at the age of 137. Abraham's other son, Isaac, waited until he was 40 years old to get married. When he married Rebekah, they found out she was barren and could not have children. Isaac interceded to God, and his wife gave birth to twins. Then as Jacob and Esau grew up super-fast in this chapter, Esau sold his birthright for a bowl of stew because he was hungry. Is that a busy enough chapter for you?

The one thing I believe God wants us to get out of this chapter is the power of prayer and in particular, intercessory prayer. Rebekah was barren in her womb. The actual verbiage is that her "womb was dead." However, when Isaac entreated the Lord and interceded on her behalf, God turned her barrenness around and she gave birth to twins. If something is fruitless or unproductive in your life, use the power of prayer to reverse the curse. If you know someone who is spinning their spiritual wheels and going nowhere, begin to intercede on their behalf, and believe God for them to begin to produce. Whatever you make happen by praying for others, God will make happen for you.

USE THE POWER OF PRAYER IN 2025

EXODUS 25
Give to God

God spoke with Moses on the mountain and gave him detailed instructions on how to build a sanctuary, or tabernacle, where He would dwell among the people. The Lord spoke to Moses telling him to take up an offering to build a holy place. There is a direct link between your heart and your money. If God has your heart, then God has your wallet. Your money is a reflection of your heart. Where and how you spend your money shows what you truly value.

"Where your treasure is, there your heart will be also". Matthew 6:21

Money and time are two commodities people use to show what is important to them. Money is one of the most talked about subjects in the entire Bible, yet people get offended over the taking up of offerings. Giving money to the place where you get spiritually fed helps:

- To pay the bills of the church
- To pay the staff members a salary
- To provide maintenance and upkeep
- To buy toilet paper, make copies off a printer, get a computer to keep records, and other supplies needed for the church business to run smoothly
- To evangelize the local area and world
- Feed the hungry and help provide for the poor

Those are just a few of the things that the money is used for when you give to the church.

If God Has Your Heart,
He Has Your Wallet

As a church, we need to always progress, and it takes money to do that. Money is not evil; it is the love of money that is wrong. The Bible actually says in Ecclesiastes 10:19, that *"money answereth all things."* Do not be greedy and disobedient concerning your giving to God. Give to God through the vehicle of the church, then God will reward you.

GIVE FINANCES TO GOD IN 2025!!!

LEVITICUS 25
Reset Your Life

This chapter in the Bible describes the Year of Jubilee which was a time of celebration and freedom that the Israelites were to observe every 50 years. The Year of Jubilee was proclaimed with the blowing of the ram's horn on the Day of Atonement. There were three main things that happened that brought great joy to the people:

1. Debts were forgiven.
2. Slaves were freed.
3. Property was returned to the rightful owner.

The Year of Jubilee was a law established by God to give the people a chance to basically reset their lives. In every area including economically, culturally, relationally, financially, environmentally, and spiritually, the people were given an opportunity to begin again and start again. This year of 2025 God is giving us a chance to reset our lives. Jubilee celebrations usually only happen once in a person's lifetime, so take advantage of this incredible moment in history. God has already done His job. Now it is up to you to reevaluate the things in your life that need improvement. Ask yourself questions like ….

- What can I do to improve my health?
- What do I need to do to get out of debt?
- What is holding me back from totally surrendering to God?

- How can I be a better spouse?
- Who do I need to forgive?

Those are just a few questions you need to ask and answer honestly to begin the reset in your life. This could be the best year of your life and set you up for blessing the rest of your life. God's will for your life is jubilee and joy, so begin to reset your life today.

RESET YOUR LIFE IN 2025!!!

NUMBERS 25
Boldness to Speak Out

Numbers 25 tells the story of the Israelites' sin of idolatry and the punishment they received. They were sexually enticed by the Moabite women and led into idolatry to worship their false god, Baal. Their sexual sin was even taking place at the door of the Tabernacle. A man by the name of Phinehas was so appalled at the disrespect towards God and the church that he actually killed them both for their rebellious actions that took place in front of the church.

Now, I am not suggesting or encouraging anyone to go and kill somebody because they are disgusted by the sin that is happening in the church and in the world. What I am saying is, it is time to speak out against sin. Silence is not golden, and boldness is required from the child of God. Phinehas was the grandson of Aaron, and his actions stopped the plague after 24,000 people were killed to earn God's favor. Have the courage to speak up and speak out against sin in the church and in the world. Do not be so angry that the sin of others drives you to sin yourself, but live a righteous life. Do not be silent about speaking out against sin. Sin will take you where you do not want to go, cost you more than you are willing to pay, and keep you there longer than you want to stay.

BOLDNESS TO SPEAK UP AND OUT
AGAINST SIN IN 2025!!!

DEUTERONOMY 25
Vote for Godly Principles

This chapter addresses the issues that deal with the laws of God on how to properly and correctly coexist with one another. Deuteronomy 25 talks about being fair in our business dealings and how to have healthy relationships with others. It mentions how we must be honest, responsible, and always act with integrity. It also addresses a lot of political issues like poverty, war, homelessness, capital punishment, agriculture, marriage, and the mistreatment of animals. This chapter covers so many relevant issues that we are still dealing with thousands of years after Moses wrote these words. In America, we are too caught up in identifying with a certain political party. As Christians, we fail to remember it is not about democratic or republican ideology; it is about Biblical values. Always choose godly principles over secular politics. We should vote for policies that are mentioned in the Bible, not for people who make promises they do not keep. This is a year we must make choices based upon God's Word and not a political affiliation. Do not be a republican or democratic, be a Christian who votes on Biblical values and principles. If God is for something, then we are for that something. If God is against something, then we are against that something. Make sure your political beliefs line up with your godly beliefs.

VOTE FOR GODLY PRINCIPLES IN 2025!!!

If God is for Something, We Are for It
If God is Against Something, We Are Against It

---

1 SAMUEL 25
Be A Peacemaker

This chapter introduces us to one of the female heroes in the Bible, Abigail. She was not just a hero, she was a shero because people of valor can be male or female.

When Abigail's husband, Nabal, responds to David's request for food with rudeness and pride, Abigail takes action to be a peacemaker when David wants revenge. Abigail is a Biblical role model of courage and peacemaking for all people, not just women. Abigail was able to smooth out a confrontation between two leaders that would have been destructive.

Six Characteristics That Made Abigail a Peacemaker

1. Full of Wisdom
2. Persuasive Speaker
3. Good Listener
4. Patient
5. Problem-Solver
6. Kindness & Gentleness

"Blessed are the peacemakers, for they will be called children of God," Matthew 5:9

Abigail teaches us the value of keeping our composure, seeing the bigger picture, forming a workable plan, and influencing people to follow a peaceful solution. Ask God to give the influence to persuade others to make you a better peacemaker among people.

BE A PEACEMAKER IN 2025!!!

2 KINGS 25

Consider the Consequences Before Acting

This is the only book in the Bible that has exactly 25 chapters which is reason enough to pay extra attention to these words. 2 Kings 25 in the Bible describes the fall of Jerusalem and the exile of Judah after years of disobedience to God. Their disobedience led to:

1. Jerusalem experiencing famine
2. King Zedekiah being captured and taken hostage
3. The Temple, royal palace, and a lot of the houses of Israel being burned to the ground
4. The last of Solomon's gold and silver being taken

This chapter teaches us that our actions have consequences. One thing we as Christians must do better is think before we act and be led by the Spirit, not by the flesh. You know you are in the flesh when you act without considering the cost and consequences of your actions. Disobedience brings death. Obedience brings life.

CONSIDER THE CONSEQUENCES IN 2025!!!

Disobedience Brings Death
Obedience Brings Life

---

1 CHRONICLES 25
Worship God

David loved music and was personally involved in organizing singers and instrumentalists. Out of the 38,000 Levites that existed in David's day, only 4,000 were set apart to praise the Lord with musical instruments (1 Chronicles 23:5), and 288 were chosen as singers in the Temple (1 Chronicles 25:7). In order to be chosen to be part of the praise and worship team, they had to have two things:

1. An ability to play or sing.
2. An anointing from God to play or sing.

They were not only to lead people into the presence of God, but their true calling was to touch the heart of God and release His glory from heaven to earth.

David understood that worship is:

1. Intimacy with God
2. The way to release the supernatural
3. The key to tilling up the hard soil of our hearts is to prepare it for the Word of God to be planted
4. How the gifts of God get unlocked
5. How wounds are healed
6. How curses are broken
7. Required to please the Lord
8. What we are called to do as Christians

We declared 2024 as the Year of Worship, and the worship of God must continue throughout 2025. We are called to be worshipers, whether we have a beautiful voice to sing or not, whether we are talented enough to play an instrument or not. We are all called to worship God in spirit and in truth.

WORSHIP GOD IN 2025!!!

2 CHRONICLES 25
Motives Matter

This is a chapter about King Amaziah who was twenty-five years old when he became king, and he reigned twenty-nine years in Jerusalem. All you need to know about Amaziah is found in 2 Chronicles 25:2 (ESV), *"And he did what was right in the eyes of the LORD, yet not with a whole heart."*

God wants more from His people than a shallow-level, half-hearted relationship. Amaziah did what was right, but he did not do it with his whole heart. He was half-hearted in his commitment to God and his motives were wrong. This verse challenges believers to examine their hearts and motivations to seek wholehearted devotion to God. Amaziah went through the motions, but his outward actions did not line up with his inward motivations. Our motives for serving and loving the Lord should be selfless, not selfish.

36

"People may be pure in their own eyes, but the LORD examines their motives." Proverbs 16:2 (NLT)

"When you ask, you do not receive, because you ask with wrong motives, that you may spend what you get on your pleasures." James 4:3 (NIV)

How to Have Pure Motives

1. Be driven to do good by love, not duty.
2. Seek to glorify God, not yourself.
3. Do right without recognition or reward.
4. Desire to motivate, not manipulate.

Your motives matter and God wants all of you, not some of you. Check your actions to make sure your motives are correct. It is not just "what you do", it is "why you are doing it" that really matters.

YOUR MOTIVES MATTER IN 2025!!!

JOB 25
Draw a Circle; Do Not Point Fingers

Job 25 is Bildad's third and final speech to Job, which is nothing more than another attempt to convince Job that he has brought all these problems upon himself because of some hidden sin in his life. This is a small, six-verse chapter where his so-called friend says a whole lot of nothing. Bildad is getting frustrated with his lack of ability to convince Job of his wrongdoings and basically calls him a "worm." A worm lives in dirt and does not have any limbs, so Bildad is referring to Job's defense of his character in chapter 24. He is saying that Job's argument is so bad that he is dirty in God's eyes and does not have a leg to stand on when it comes to his defense. Bildad is convinced that he is right and that Job is wrong. Bildad is not only falsely judging Job, but he is also not offering any hope, grace, or love. The Bible warns us against judging others:

> *"Do not judge, or you too will be judged. For in the same way you judge others, you will be judged, and with the measure you use, it will be measured to you." Matthew 7:1-2* (NIV)

The Bible also encourages us to get the 2x4 out of our eyes before getting the speck out of other people's eyes. This is a year to draw a circle around yourself and focus on what you need to do to improve yourself. Pointing the finger at others and acting like you have been deputized as God's spiritual police to reveal the flaws of others, is not only wrong, it is hypocritical. Pray for others and improve yourself. You would be better served to literally "MYOB" or Mind Your Own Business.

DRAW A CIRCLE, DO NOT POINT FINGERS
AT OTHERS IN 2025!!!

PSALM 25
Trust God

This Psalm teaches us to not stop believing in God just because life becomes hard. God is God on the mountain and God is God in the valley. David is praying for four things in Psalm 25:

1. Remove the shame from past sins, v.2-3
2. Wisdom and guidance, v.4-5
3. God's forgiveness and forgetfulness, v.6-11
4. Deliverance from evil intentions of others, v.15-18

Psalm 25 is a great psalm because it teaches us to pray for specific things that most of us deal with, such as removing shame, the need for wisdom, forgiveness, and deliverance. These are all important issues that Christians ought to be praying to God about and asking for help. David reminds us that whether we are facing an inward battle with our emotions or an outer battle with our enemies, we can trust God in good and bad times.

TRUST GOD IN GOOD TIMES AND
BAD TIMES IN 2025!!!

---

*God is God on The Mountain,
and God is God in The Valley*

PROVERBS 25
New Year's Commitments

This is a proverb from Solomon that was found 270 years after Solomon's death by King Hezekiah's people and published for their benefit. 1 Kings 4:32 tells us that Solomon spoke three thousand proverbs. So, all of Solomon's wisdom is not included in the Book of Proverbs. However, Proverbs 25 gives us commitments that we need to make to God in 2025.

20 New Year Commitments For 2025

1. Search the Word, v.2-3
2. Purge All Impurities, v.4
3. Never Compromise, v.5
4. Avoid Self-Exaltation, v.6-7
5. Be Discreet About Solutions, v.8-10
6. Use Words Wisely, v.11-12
7. Minister Upwards, v.13
8. Do Not Brag, v.14
9. Be Patient, v.15
10. Do Not Overindulge, v.16
11. Never Overstay Your Welcome, v.17
12. Be Faithful, v.18-19
13. Be Sensitive to the Hurting, v.20
14. Bless Those That Curse You, v.21-22
15. Avoid Anger, v.23
16. Seek Peace in Your Marriage, v.24
17. Be An Encourager, v.25

18. Do Not Bring Disgrace Upon God, v.26
19. Do Not Do Things for Attention, v.27
20. Control Yourself, v.28

Start the year off correctly and ensure you have a successful year by following these new year commitments all 365 days of 2025.

KEEP YOUR COMMITMENTS IN 2025!!!

ISAIAH 25
The Great Banquet

This is one of the shortest chapters in the Book of Isaiah, but it is also one of the most prophetic. It starts with Isaiah celebrating the faithfulness and deliverance of God. Isaiah praises God for three things:

1. For protecting the poor and needy
2. For miraculous power
3. For delivering Israel from oppression

Then Isaiah prophesied about a banquet to be hosted by God for the church, or His bride, that the New Testament refers to as the "marriage supper of the lamb" in Revelation 19:9. There Jesus will reward those who have been faithful to Him. Jesus is so looking forward to this banquet, or award ceremony, that He said to His disciples at the Last Supper:

"I will not drink of this fruit of the vine from now on until that day when I drink it new with you in My Father's kingdom" Matthew 26:29

Isaiah declares that Jesus will do seven wonderful things at this banquet:

1. There will be a huge meal with all kinds of delicious food to eat.
2. Jesus will destroy evil.
3. Jesus will swallow up death forever.
4. Jesus will marry His bride, which is the church.
5. Jesus will wipe the tears from our eyes.
6. The church will be given its final correction.
7. All things will be resolved.

Wow! Make sure you do everything you can to walk in right standing with God and receive an invitation to the greatest banquet or party of all time.

LET THE CHURCH ARISE AND PREPARE FOR THE
GREAT BANQUET IN 2025!!!

JEREMIAH 25
Be Submissive, Not Stubborn

Jeremiah is bringing a message of God's judgment and the consequences of disobedience because of Judah's rebellion. Jeremiah prophesies that Judah will be conquered by Babylon and exiled to Babylon for 70 years. Jeremiah suggests the severity of judgment is determined by the severity of the rebellion. Rebellion is defined as an act of open resistance to authority. It may seem like an overstatement, but rebellion against God is spiritual terrorism. God wants to get our attention and have us get serious about removing rebellion from our lives.

Five Facts About Rebellion

1. The devil led a rebellion against God in heaven, Isaiah 14:12-15
2. Rebellion is connected to witchcraft, 1 Samuel 15:23
3. Rebellion is deadly, Proverbs 17:11
4. Rebellion begins in the heart, Hebrews 3:8
5. Rebellion is one of the major sins of the end-times, Jude 1:11

Rebellion Against God Is Spiritual Terrorism

To understand what rebellion is, we might need to know what the opposite of rebellion is. The opposite of rebellion is submission, compliance, and obedience. God wants us to be submissive, not stubborn. So, pray for God to help you be submissive, compliant, and obedient throughout this year.

BE SUBMISSIVE, NOT STUBBORN IN 2025!!!

Ezekiel 25

Pray for Peace in Israel

Ezekiel begins to shift the focus of judgment off of Israel to its neighbors. He prophesied against Ammon, Moab, Edom, and Philistia because they all trusted in other gods. They had become pagan nations that turned against the true God. Their actions eventually caused God to punish them for all their deeds. The judgment of God came to these other nations because:

1. They rejoiced over Israel's downfall.
2. They mocked and stole from God's people.
3. They constantly oppressed and harassed Israel.

With everything that Israel has gone through, it is more important than ever to pray for the peace of Jerusalem and all of Israel. We need to be friends with the Jewish people and Israel in order for us to have God's favor on us.

"But if you truly obey his voice and do all that I say, then I will be an enemy to your enemies and an adversary to your adversaries" Exodus 23:22 (NIV)

When you are an enemy of the Jews and Israel, you are an enemy of God.

PRAY FOR PEACE IN ISRAEL AND AGAINST
ANTI-SEMITISM IN 2025!!!

MATTHEW 25
Be Prepared

Jesus is trying to prepare His people for the final judgment by teaching that at the time of His second coming, only those who are prepared shall be allowed to enter into His Kingdom. We as Christians can fail to enter the Kingdom of God by being unprepared. As in the parable of the ten virgins, we need to be prepared for the unexpected. We need to be prepared for the return of Jesus at any time. In the parable of the talents, we will be judged based on how ready we are to use the gifts that God has entrusted to us to help others. Generally, Jesus is telling us we will have to answer for how well or poorly we treated others who were in need. It is so important to be ready and available. Your greatest ability is availability!!!

45

Being prepared is about three things:

1. Being ready to be used for God's glory
2. Being willing to be used for God's glory
3. Being available to be used for God's glory

Ready, willing, and available are the keys to being prepared to be successful and help others succeed. God will provide the ability; you provide the availability.

BE PREPARED IN 2025!!!

ACTS 25
Dealing with False Accusations

Paul finds himself on trial for his life, having already served two years in prison for something he did not do. He was being falsely charged. He is not pouting or looking for revenge; Paul is patiently waiting on God's provision.

Be ready and be aware that false accusations will come in 2025. They will come to destroy people in the church, political arena, and those who are attempting to straighten up the crooked things in this world. Paul said if

I am wrong, and you can prove I committed crimes that deserve the death penalty, then go ahead and take my life. The leaders and religious people could not even put into words what he did wrong, let alone find anyone to convict him. Just because someone makes a claim or says it on the internet, does not mean it is true. Do not rush to judgment, and do not believe everything you hear or read. There must be proof and verifiable facts, not just accusations. It is important to respond properly, according to God's Word, when we get falsely accused.

How to Properly React When Falsely Accused

1. Stay calm, do not be defensive.
2. Consider the source.
3. If possible, provide evidence that the accusation is false.
4. Forgive your accuser.
5. Move forward.
6. Ask God for vindication.

Being falsely accused is unfair, hurtful, and can be costly. We can never control others, but we can control ourselves, so it is important to always respond in a correct manner. Two wrongs do not make a right, so learn to react right even when others act wrong.

RESPOND CORRECTLY TO FALSE
ACCUSATIONS IN 2025!!!

Chapter 25's Summary

Genesis 25 = The Power of Prayer

Exodus 25 = Give to God

Leviticus 25 = Reset Your Life

Numbers 25 = Boldness to Speak Out

Deuteronomy 25 = Vote for Godly Principles

1 Samuel 25 = Be a Peacemaker

2 Kings 25 = Consider the Consequences

1 Chronicles 25 = Worship God

2 Chronicles 25 = Motives Matter

Job 25 = Draw a Circle; Do Not Point Fingers

Psalm 25 = Trust God

Proverbs 25 = New Year's Commitments

Isaiah 25 = The Great Banquet

Jeremiah 25 = Be Submissive, Not Stubborn

Ezekiel 25 = Pray for Peace in Israel

Matthew 25 = Be Prepared

Acts 25 = Respond Correctly to False Accusations

Chapter 5
Prophetic Scriptures for 2025

Scriptures That Mention Twenty-Five

Serve the Lord

"This is it that belongeth unto the Levites: from twenty and five years old and upward they shall go in to wait upon the service of the tabernacle of the congregation:" Numbers 8:24

    In the Old Testament, you had to be 25 years old to begin serving the Lord in the Tabernacle. Now it is more about spiritual maturity than your natural age. We need to encourage our youth to be involved in the church and use their gifts, sooner rather than later, to build the Kingdom of God. No matter our age, let us be passionate about our pursuit of God in 2025.

Let God's Grace Reign

"Jehoshaphat was thirty and five years old when he began to reign; and he reigned twenty and five years in Jerusalem. And his mother's name was Azubah the daughter of Shilhi." 1 Kings 22:42

"He was twenty and five years old when he began to reign, and reigned twenty and nine years in Jerusalem. And his mother's name was Jehoaddan of Jerusalem."
2 Kings 14:2

"Five and twenty years old was he when he began to reign, and he reigned sixteen years in Jerusalem. And his mother's name was Jerusha, the daughter of Zadok."
2 Kings 15:33

"Twenty and five years old was he when he began to reign; and he reigned twenty and nine years in Jerusalem. His mother's name also was Abi, the daughter of Zachariah."
2 Kings 18:2

"Jehoiakim was twenty and five years old when he began to reign; and he reigned eleven years in Jerusalem. And his mother's name was Zebudah, the daughter of Pedaiah of Rumah." 2 Kings 23:36

"And Jehoshaphat reigned over Judah: he was thirty and five years old when he began to reign, and he reigned twenty and five years in Jerusalem. And his mother's name was Azubah the daughter of Shilhi." 2 Chronicles 20:31

"Amaziah was twenty and five years old when he began to reign, and he reigned twenty and nine years in Jerusalem. And his mother's name was Jehoaddan of Jerusalem."
2 Chronicles 25:1

"Jotham was twenty and five years old when he began to reign, and he reigned sixteen years in Jerusalem. His mother's name also was Jerushah, the daughter of Zadok." 2 Chronicles 27:1

"He was five and twenty years old when he began to reign, and reigned sixteen years in Jerusalem."
2 Chronicles 27:8

"Hezekiah began to reign when he was five and twenty years old, and he reigned nine and twenty years in Jerusalem. And his mother's name was Abijah, the daughter of Zechariah." 2 Chronicles 29:1

"Jehoiakim was twenty and five years old when he began to reign, and he reigned eleven years in Jerusalem: and he did that which was evil in the sight of the Lord his God."
2 Chronicles 36:5

Eleven of the 23 times the number 25 is mentioned revolves around a certain king's reign. The word reign is a reference to how they started to reign at 25 years of age or how they reigned for 25 years. Jesus is the King of Kings and the Lord of Lords. He needs to reign and rule in our lives in 2025. Since we are declaring this to be a Year of Grace, let the grace of God reign in our lives throughout this year.

Worship God

"And he brought me into the inner court of the Lord's house, and, behold, at the door of the temple of the Lord, between the porch and the altar, were about five and twenty men, with their backs toward the temple of the

Lord, and their faces toward the east; and they worshipped the sun toward the east." Ezekiel 8:16

The Year of Worship for 2024 continues in 2025. What we worship is what we value. Place a high value on God by placing a high value on worshiping God in 2025.

Spiritual Elevation

"Moreover the spirit lifted me up, and brought me unto the east gate of the Lord's house, which looketh eastward: and behold at the door of the gate five and twenty men; among whom I saw Jaazaniah the son of Azur, and Pelatiah the son of Benaiah, princes of the people." Ezekiel 11:1

Do not settle for ankle-deep, knee-deep, or waist-deep waters when God has more for you in 2025. Get into waters that you cannot hold, but where only God can hold you. Let God promote, raise, advance, and cause you to flourish in your life this year. Awake and celebrate because your fate is to elevate in 2025.

Awake and Celebrate Because
Your Fate is to Elevate

Be Deliberate About Following Directions

"He measured then the gate from the roof of one little chamber to the roof of another: the breadth was five and twenty cubits, door against door." Ezekiel 40:13

"And the little chambers thereof were three on this side and three on that side; and the posts thereof and the arches thereof were after the measure of the first gate: the length thereof was fifty cubits, and the breadth five and twenty cubits." Ezekiel 40:21

"And there were windows in it and in the arches thereof round about, like those windows: the length was fifty cubits, and the breadth five and twenty cubits." Ezekiel 40:25

"And the little chambers thereof, and the posts thereof, and the arches thereof, according to these measures: and there were windows in it and in the arches thereof round about: it was fifty cubits long, and five and twenty cubits broad." Ezekiel 40:29

"And the arches round about were five and twenty cubits long, and five cubits broad." Ezekiel 40:30

"And the little chambers thereof, and the posts thereof, and the arches thereof, were according to these measures: and there were windows therein and in the arches thereof round about: it was fifty cubits long, and five and twenty cubits broad." Ezekiel 40:33

"The little chambers thereof, the posts thereof, and the arches thereof, and the windows to it round about: the length was fifty cubits, and the breadth five and twenty cubits." Ezekiel 40:36

"And the shekel shall be twenty gerahs: twenty shekels, five and twenty shekels, fifteen shekels, shall be your maneh." Ezekiel 45:12

Eight times when the number 25 is mentioned in the Bible, it revolves around following detailed instructions. God wants things to be done specifically, precisely, and correctly, so we must listen and follow God's detailed instructions. God gave Israel specific directions to follow when it came to the dimensions of building the Tabernacle. Be deliberate to follow the direction of God, and never modify God's original instructions. Do not deviate from the details in 2025.

Miracles

"So when they had rowed about five and twenty or thirty furlongs, they see Jesus walking on the sea, and drawing nigh unto the ship: and they were afraid." John 6:19

According to John, Jesus walked on water for 25-30 furlongs to get to His disciples in the middle of the storm. This is a year of miracles where Jesus will demonstrate His glory to His disciples and do whatever He needs to do to manifest His power in 2025.

Build an Altar

"And if thou wilt make me an altar of stone, thou shalt not build it of hewn stone: for if thou lift up thy tool upon it, thou hast polluted it." Exodus 20:25

Altars are special places where we learn not only to acknowledge, approach, and appreciate God, but also where we make personal sacrifices unto the Lord.

Cleanliness

"Ye shall therefore put difference between clean beasts and unclean, and between unclean fowls and clean: and ye shall not make your souls abominable by beast, or by fowl, or by any manner of living thing that creepeth on the ground, which I have separated from you as unclean." Leviticus 20:25

Cleanliness is required by God both on the outside, to prevent disease, and on the inside, to please the Lord.

Go Higher

"Take Aaron and Eleazar his son, and bring them up unto mount Hor:" Numbers 20:25

Do not settle for less than God's best. Go deeper, further, and higher in 2025.

Be a Peacemaker

"And Benjamin went forth against them out of Gibeah the second day, and destroyed down to the ground of the children of Israel again eighteen thousand men; all these drew the sword." Judges 20:25

Peacemakers prevent conflicts, mediate disputes, solve problems, and bring reconciliation to those who are walking in division.

Loyalty

"And the king sat upon his seat, as at other times, even upon a seat by the wall: and Jonathan arose, and Abner sat by Saul's side, and David's place was empty." 1 Samuel 20:25

Loyalty is about faithfulness, dedication, devotion, and unswerving allegiance to another. Make sure your loyalty towards the Lord is visible in 2025.

Journal

"And Sheva was scribe: and Zadok and Abiathar were the priests:" 2 Samuel 20:25

Write down, document, and keep a record of all the victories that God is going to do in 2025.

Strength

"And number thee an army, like the army that thou hast lost, horse for horse, and chariot for chariot: and we will fight against them in the plain, and surely we shall be stronger than they. And he hearkened unto their voice, and did so." 1 Kings 20:25

The Bible makes it very clear that it is not by might, nor by power, but by His Spirit. If you need strength, go to the Lord and get Holy Ghost power.

Bountiful Blessings

"And when Jehoshaphat and his people came to take away the spoil of them, they found among them in abundance both riches with the dead bodies, and precious jewels, which they stripped off for themselves, more than they could carry away: and they were three days in gathering of the spoil, it was so much." 2 Chronicles 20:25

God gave Israel so many blessings it took three full days for them to gather all of their harvest. Be prepared for God to give you open blessings and not just blessings in disguise.

Do Not Fear

"It is drawn, and cometh out of the body; yea, the glittering sword cometh out of his gall: terrors are upon him." Job 20:25

Fear is not from God, so do not activate fear; activate faith in 2025.

Do Not Activate Fear; Activate Faith

Live Holy

"It is a snare to the man who devoureth that which is holy, and after vows to make enquiry." Proverbs 20:25

Allow God to separate you from the pack and sanctify your soul, so you can be Holy as God is holy in 2025.

Do Good

"Wherefore I gave them also statutes that were not good, and judgments whereby they should not live;"
Ezekiel 20:25

Good is always God's best. Make sure you are doing good in 2025.

Dominion

"But Jesus called them unto him, and said, Ye know that the princes of the Gentiles exercise dominion over them,

and they that are great exercise authority upon them."
Matthew 20:25

This is a year for the church to walk in dominion and exercise authority over the enemy. Do not let sin or the devil dominate you. You dominate over sin and the devil.

Pay Your Taxes

"And he said unto them, Render therefore unto Caesar the things which be Caesar's, and unto God the things which be God's." Luke 20:25

Pay your taxes and obey the laws of the land to be in the right standing with God in 2025.

Verification

"The other disciples therefore said unto him, We have seen the Lord. But he said unto them, Except I shall see in his hands the print of the nails, and put my finger into the print of the nails, and thrust my hand into his side, I will not believe." John 20:25

We are not to immediately believe or reject a prophetic word of God. We are encouraged to always judge. Judging the word means verifying the word or looking for confirmation to solidify a truth.

Preach Jesus

"And now, behold, I know that ye all, among whom I have gone preaching the kingdom of God, shall see my face no more." Acts 20:25

You might be the only Jesus some will see or hear. Make sure you are preaching the words of Jesus from the Word of God.

You Might be the Only Jesus People Meet

25:25 Scriptures

Do Not Be a Sell Out

"And the first came out red, all over like an hairy garment; and they called his name Esau." Genesis 25:25

A sellout is a person who compromises their personal values or integrity for money or personal advancement. Be honorable in all you do in 2025.

Set Boundaries

"And thou shalt make unto it a border of an hand breadth round about, and thou shalt make a golden crown to the border thereof round about." Exodus 25:25

Setting boundaries communicates to others what is acceptable and what is not acceptable to you as a person. Setting and enforcing boundaries is key to successful relationships.

Have Compassion

"If thy brother be waxen poor, and hath sold away some of his possession, and if any of his kin come to redeem it, then shall he redeem that which his brother sold." Leviticus 25:25

Compassion is the feeling of sadness and sympathy for someone else's suffering that is accompanied by a desire to help others. Helping others is helping yourself in 2025.

Be a Peacemaker

"Let not my lord, I pray thee, regard this man of Belial, even Nabal: for as his name is, so is he; Nabal is his name, and folly is with him: but I thine handmaid saw not the young men of my lord, whom thou didst send." 1 Samuel 25:25

Abigail was a humble servant who sought peace, not war. Be a peacemaker, not a troublemaker in 2025.

Royalty

"But it came to pass in the seventh month, that Ishmael the son of Nethaniah, the son of Elishama, of the seed royal, came, and ten men with him, and smote Gedaliah, that he died, and the Jews and the Chaldees that were with him at Mizpah". 2 Kings 25:25

The Bible declares your gift has the potential to bring you before kings. Use your gifts in 2025.

Grace

"The eighteenth to Hanani, he, his sons, and his brethren, were twelve:" 1 Chronicles 25:25

Hanani means God is gracious, so God is expecting His children to offer grace to others, the way God has offered grace to them.

Live Life

"And Amaziah the son of Joash king of Judah lived after the death of Joash son of Jehoahaz king of Israel fifteen years." 2 Chronicles 25:25

Living life is about living life in the moment and living life to the fullest. Make the most of your time on Earth in 2025.

Encourage Others

"As cold waters to a thirsty soul, so is good news from a far country." Proverbs 25:25

Send a message of hope and blessing to someone you know who you have not heard from in a long time. Be an encourager in 2025.

Use Your Gifts

"And I was afraid, and went and hid thy talent in the earth: lo, there thou hast that is thine." Matthew 25:25

Do not be afraid to use your God-given gifts to build God's Kingdom in 2025.

Make Right Judgment

"But when I found that he had committed nothing worthy of death, and that he himself hath appealed to Augustus, I have determined to send him." Acts 25:25

The quality of your life is determined by the quality of your decisions. Be wise in 2025.

Chapter 6
Spiritual Forecast

The beginning of every new year springs forth a freshness from above as we reflect on our past, consider our present, and have hope for what the future will bring. *"You are living in unprecedented times of uncertainty and division. You are treading in uncharted territory where you do not have all the answers. It is time to yield to the Lord and quit trying to fix problems or achieve progress on your own. You have allowed stubbornness and stiff-neckedness to rule your life, which has created a schism that has produced a great divide. You have sought justice and have been motivated by the punishment of others to the point you have put yourself in the position of judge and jury. You are operating outside of your jurisdiction. You are meddling in affairs that are not yours to travel in. You are trespassing on territory you should avoid, and you are violating My orders and commands. This is a new year with a new vision. As the calendar has changed, so must your approach to building My Kingdom change. Your opinions, your lack of empathy, your pride, and your desire to always be right have hindered you from being who I desire you to be. It has kept you from doing what I need you to do. As you look in a mirror and see flaws, look into My Word and allow it to reveal My will for 2025. The best gift I offer to mankind is the gift I want you to offer to others this year. The best gift is .... Grace."*

Stop expecting things from others that you cannot do or give yourselves. You give grace, you will get grace. Let this be Year of Grace. So, what is giving grace to others all about?

- It is about forgiveness instead of holding a grudge.
- It is about unconditional love.
- It is about understanding instead of being understood.
- It is about compassion.
- It is about giving them a break when they do something wrong.
- It is about showing them favor even when they do not deserve it.
- It is about choosing to be kind instead of judging.
- It is about being patient with others' shortcomings.
- It is about giving someone the benefit of the doubt.
- It is about supporting others when they are struggling with things you may not be aware of.
- It is about being patient when you want to get angry.
- It is about believing the best instead of assuming the worst.
- It is about giving someone a second chance.
- It is about giving somebody a free pass.
- It is about keeping your mouth shut when you want to say something you should not.
- It is about walking in humility, not pride.
- It is about sharing the Good News with someone who is in bad shape.

- It is about a hand-up, not a hand-out.
- It is about encouraging others when you are discouraged yourself.
- It is about accepting the fact it is ok not to be perfect.
- It is about not making everything such a big deal.
- It is about going the extra mile.
- It is about turning the other cheek.
- It is about grasping that others can have a bad day.
- It is about giving something away to others that you will one day need for yourself.

---

*Grace Is About Keeping Your Mouth Shut
When You Want to Say Something You
Should Not*

As much as it is important to understand what grace is, it is also important to understand what grace is not …

- It is not a free pass to do whatever you want without consequences.
- It is not a license to sin.
- It is not compromising your belief system.
- It is not an excuse to sin.
- It is not infinite; it will one day come to an end.
- It is not earned by works.
- It is not a favor; it is the favor of God.
- It is not about fairness.

- It is not a substitute for sanctification.
- It is not easy to give to others.
- It is not about just giving it to others, it is also about giving it to yourself.
- It is not about leniency or clemency.
- It is not a permission slip from heaven to not live up to your God-given destiny.
- It is not some divine tolerance.
- It is not for the godly as much as it is for the ungodly.
- It is not a reason to be lazy and put no effort into controlling your flesh.
- It is not about lowering the spiritual bar.

Grace is not just a characteristic of God; it is God. God is Grace. *"You will be tested this year, and this may be the toughest examination you have ever had to take, but My expectation is for you to pass the test. You cannot do this on your own, so remember My words I spoke through Zechariah, 'Not by might, nor by power, but by my Spirit.' Allow the Holy Spirit to rule your spirit, soul, and body. Love in the Spirit, live in the Spirit, give in the Spirit, pray in the Spirit, hope in the Spirit, and give grace to others in the Spirit. You cannot allow the fleshly patterns you have created in the past to keep you from experiencing the spiritual prosperity I have for you in your future. You have done it your way long enough, and My judgment will come soon enough, but for now, it is all about grace in 2025."*

States in the Northeast Region and Their Specific "Word" for 2025:

Connecticut – Agreement
Delaware – Love
Maine – Stability
Maryland – Rebuke
Massachusetts – Breakthrough
New Hampshire – Provision
New Jersey – Deliverance
New York – Rest
Pennsylvania – Leadership
Rhode Island – Integrity
Vermont – Bondage

Prayer for the Northeast Region:

"Prayer for Our Government"
By George Washington

I now make it my earnest prayer, that God would have you, and the state over which you preside, in His holy protection, that He would incline the hearts of the citizens to cultivate a spirit of subordination and obedience to government, to entertain a brotherly affection and love for one another, for their fellow citizens of the United States at large, and particularly for their brethren who have served in the field, and finally, that He would most graciously be pleased to dispose us all, to do justice, to love mercy, and to demean ourselves with that charity, humility, and pacific temper of mind, which were the characteristics of the Divine Author of our blessed religion, and without an humble imitation of whose example in these things, we can never hope to be a happy nation.

Book of the Bible for the Northeast Region:
Philemon

Scripture for the Northeast Region:
"Moreover the law entered, that the offence might abound. But where sin abounded, grace did much more abound:" Romans 5:20

State in the Northeast Region to Watch:
Pennsylvania

Major City in the Northeast Region to Watch:
Bridgeport, Connecticut

Key Months for the Northeast Region:
February, July, October

States in the Southeast Region and Their Specific "Word" for 2025:

Alabama – Courage
Florida – Resurrection
Georgia – Kindness
Kentucky – Devotion
Mississippi – Mercy
North Carolina – Forgiveness
South Carolina – Purity
Tennessee – Persistence
Virginia – Patience
West Virginia – Change

Prayer for the Southeast Region:

"Serenity Prayer"
By Reinhold Niebuhr

God, grant me the serenity
to accept the things I cannot change,
the courage to change the things I can,
and the wisdom to know the difference.
Living one day at a time,
enjoying one moment at a time;
accepting hardship as a pathway to peace;

taking, as Jesus did,
this sinful world as it is,
not as I would have it;
trusting that You will make all things right
if I surrender to Your will;
so that I may be reasonably happy in this life
and supremely happy with You forever in the next.
Amen.

Book of the Bible for the Southeast Region:
Jude

Scripture for the Southeast Region:
"Let us therefore come boldly unto the throne of grace, that we may obtain mercy, and find grace to help in time of need." Hebrews 4:16

State in the Southeast Region to Watch:
Tennessee

Major City in the Southeast Region to Watch:
Atlanta, Georgia

Key Months for the Southeast Region:
May, August, November

States in the Midwest Region and Their Specific "Word" for 2025:

Illinois – Truth
Indiana – Promise
Iowa – Blessed
Kansas – Faith
Michigan – Spirit
Minnesota – Peace
Missouri – Boldness
Nebraska – Covenant
North Dakota – Atonement
Ohio – Jubilee
South Dakota – Wisdom
Wisconsin – Repent

Prayer for the Midwest Region:

"Do It Anyway"
As Made Famous by Mother Teresa

People are often unreasonable, irrational, and self-centered.
Forgive them anyway.
If you are kind, people may accuse you of selfish, ulterior motives.
Be kind anyway.

If you are successful, you will win some unfaithful friends and some genuine enemies.
Succeed anyway.
If you are honest and sincere people may deceive you.
Be honest and sincere anyway.
What you spend years creating, others could destroy overnight.
Create anyway.
If you find serenity and happiness, some may be jealous.
Be happy anyway.
The good you do today, will often be forgotten.
Do good anyway.
Give the best you have, and it will never be enough.
Give your best anyway.
In the final analysis, it is between you and God.
It was never between you and them anyway.

Book of the Bible for the Midwest Region:
Ezekiel

Scripture for the Midwest Region:
"And of his fulness have all we received, and grace for grace." John 1:16

State in the Midwest Region to Watch:
Minnesota

Major City in the Midwest Region to Watch:
Fargo, North Dakota

Key Months for the Midwest Region:
March, June, September

---

*Deal With the Potential of People,
Not the Past of People*

Southwest Region

States in the Southwest Region and Their Specific "Word" for 2025:

Arizona – Grace
Arkansas – Intercede
Colorado – Health
Louisiana – Discipleship
New Mexico – Reverence
Oklahoma – Reconciliation
Texas – Influence

Prayer for the Southwest Region:

"The Lord's Prayer"
By Jesus Of Nazareth

Our Father which art in heaven, Hallowed be thy name.
Thy kingdom come, Thy will be done in earth, as it is in heaven. Give us this day our daily bread.
And forgive us our debts, as we forgive our debtors.
And lead us not into temptation, but deliver us from evil: For thine is the kingdom, and the power, and the glory, for ever. Amen.

Book of the Bible for the Southwest Region:
1 Kings

Scripture for the Southwest Region:
"And he said unto me, My grace is sufficient for thee: for my strength is made perfect in weakness. Most gladly therefore will I rather glory in my infirmities, that the power of Christ may rest upon me." 2 Corinthians 12:9

State in the Southwest Region to Watch:
Arizona

Major City in the Southwest Region to Watch:
Santa Fe, New Mexico

Key Months for the Southwest Region:
February, July, December

<u>West Region</u>

States in the West Region and Their Specific "Word" for 2025:
Alaska – Genuine
California – Extraordinary
Hawaii – Wholeness
Idaho – Compassion
Montana – Meditation
Nevada – Consistency
Oregon – Devotion
Utah – Freedom
Washington – Tolerance
Wyoming – Discernment

Prayer for the West Region:

"Receive Grace"
By John Wesley

O God, seeing as there is in Christ Jesus an infinite fullness of all that we can want or desire, May we all receive from him, grace upon grace; grace to pardon our sins, and subdue our iniquities; to justify our persons and to sanctify our souls; and to complete that holy change, that renewal of our hearts, which will enable us to be transformed into the blessed image in which You created us. O make us all acceptable to be partakers of the inheritance of your saints in light. Amen.

Book of the Bible for the West Region:
2 Chronicles

Scripture for the West Region:
"For by grace are ye saved through faith; and that not of yourselves: it is the gift of God: Not of works, lest any man should boast." Ephesians 2:8-9

State in the West Region to Watch:
Idaho

Major City in the West Region to Watch:
Anchorage

Key Months for the West Region:
January, April, December

---

*Grace is Not a Reason to Be Lazy and Put
No Effort into Controlling Your Flesh*

The Five Regions of the United States

Northeast	Southeast	Midwest	Southwest	West
Connecticut	Alabama	Illinois	Arizona	Alaska
Delaware	Florida	Indiana	Arkansas	California
Maine	Georgia	Iowa	Colorado	Hawaii
Maryland	Kentucky	Kansas	Louisiana	Idaho
Massachusetts	Mississippi	Michigan	New Mexico	Montana
New Hampshire	North Carolina	Minnesota	Oklahoma	Nevada
New Jersey	South Carolina	Missouri	Texas	Oregon
New York	Tennessee	Nebraska		Utah
Pennsylvania	Virginia	North Dakota		Washington
Rhode Island	West Virginia	Ohio		Wyoming
Vermont		South Dakota		
		Wisconsin		

Chapter 7
25th Day People

If you have a birthday on the 25th day of any month then this chapter is specifically for you. You are going to have to work at obedience to God and put your complete trust in God to be successful. This is a year for growth and change in your spirit, soul, and body. You will grow and mature. You will also experience some changes for the betterment in your life. Everything you have gone through has brought you to this incredible moment in your life. You will begin to think more realistically instead of fantasizing about things that will not become reality. There is a stabilization in your mind that will keep you from being indecisive and cause decision-making to become easier in your life. Psalm 25 is your psalm, so read it, embrace it, and pray for a revelation of it in your life. David was concerned about his foes and his faults that were keeping him from moving into his destiny. This is a psalm that David wrote from his gut, not his head, which gives us hope that God can turn our pain into prosperity. David is actually given the secret to success in verse 14 when God tells him the mystery to manifesting God's glory is to fear the Lord. God is revealing His secrets and handing you the keys to the kingdom to unlock the power of God in your life in 2025. For those of you turning 25 in 2025, this is a special year of celebration. Your 25th birthday is known as your silver birthday. You will not receive another opportunity like this, so take advantage of this chance of a lifetime. Psalm 25 is your chapter, and your verse is Proverbs 22:4, *"By humility and the fear of the Lord are riches, and honour, and life."*

Manifest God's Glory by Fearing the Lord

The only thing that can hold you back in 2025 is … yourself. Give up, let go, and let God win. It is for your benefit, and it is to your advantage. Wealth, honor, and abundance are yours as you yield yourself to God and do things God's way.

Traits of 25th Day People

<u>Positive</u>	<u>Negative</u>
– Intellectual	– Perfectionist
– Introspective	– Stubborn
– Analytical	– Strong-Minded
– Compassionate	– Complex
– Good Listeners	– Impatient
– Reliable Friends	– Independent
– Adaptable	– Impulsive
– Loyal	– Inconsistent
– Intuitive	– Indecisive
– Great Discernment	– Overthinkers
	– Do Not Trust Easily

Ten Commandments For 25th Day People In 2025

1. Do not force a square peg into a round hole.
2. You are not called to rescue and save people from themselves.
3. Never allow what is going on around you to affect what God wants to do inside of you.
4. Be comfortable with who you are.
5. Understand sometimes you strike out in life, and other times you hit a home run in life.
6. Actions speak louder than words.
7. Do not be so prideful that you fail to ask for help.
8. Master your thoughts.
9. Improve your attitude.
10. Turn your wounds into wisdom.

Prayer For 25th Day People

Lord, help me to allow things to develop in a spiritually organic way throughout this year without me forcing the issue. Everything is going to work out for my good in 2025 without my intellectual and analytical mind trying to figure everything out. This is the year I am going to master my thoughts and control all my impulsive behavior. I am going to gain victory over everything that has claimed victory over me in the past. The wounds of my past will be used by the Lord to help me speak wisdom into the lives of others, so they can win as well. I declare over my life that I am okay with who I am, but I still want God to change me from the inside out. Improve me, oh God, so You can use me to build Your Kingdom. Let me be humble, and let my actions speak louder than my words. Give me the best year of my life and help me to give You the glory for all things in 2025.

AMEN

We have listed just some of the famous people who have birthdays on the 25th day of each month.

JANUARY

Alicia Keys, Singer
Etta James, Singer
Jenifer Lewis, Actress
Sheila Johnson, Billionaire
The Honky Tonk Man (Wayne Farris), Wrestler
Volodymyr Zelenskyy, Ukrainian President

FEBRUARY

Bobby Riggs, Tennis Player
Sally Jesse Raphael, Talk Show Host
Billy Packer, Broadcaster
George Harrison, Singer/Songwriter
Ric Flair, Wrestler
James Brown, Sportscaster
Paul O'Neill, MLB

MARCH

John Winebrenner, Church of God Founder
Eileen Ford, Modeling Agency Founder
Gloria Steinem, Feminist
Aretha Franklin, Singer
Elton John, Singer
Sarah Jessica Parker, Actress
Tom Glavine, MLB
Danica Patrick, Auto Racer

APRIL

Ella Fitzgerald, Singer
"Meadowlark" Lemon, Globetrotter
Al Pacino, Actor
Adam Silver, NBA Commissioner
Joe Buck, Sportscaster
Reneé Zellweger, Actress
Matthew West, Christian Singer

MAY

Ralph Waldo Emerson, Author
Ian McKellen, Actor
Frank Oz, Puppeteer
Mike Myers, Comedian
Octavia Spencer, Actress
Keith Hamilton, NFL
Norman Powell, NBA

JUNE

George Orwell, Author
Willis Reed, NBA
Carly Simon, Singer
Ian McDonald, Musician
Michael Sabatino, Actor
Ricky Gervais, Comedian
George Michael, Singer

JULY

Estelle Getty, Actress
Nate Thurmond, NBA
John Gibson, TV Host
Walter Payton, NFL
Matt LeBlanc, Actor
Bryce Young, NFL

AUGUST

Sean Connery, Actor
Gene Simmons, Bassist
Elvis Costello, Singer
Tim Burton, Director
Billy Ray Cyrus, Singer
Blair Underwood, Actress
Rachel Ray, TV Personality/Chef
Claudia Schiffer, Model
Marvin Harrison, NFL
Blake Lively, Actress

SEPTEMBER

Phil Rizzuto, MLB
Barbara Walters, Journalist
Michael Douglas, Actor
Cheryl Tiegs, Model
Mark Hamill, Actor
Christopher Reeve, Actor
Scottie Pippen, NBA
Will Smith, Actor
Catherine Zeta-Jones, Actress
John Lynch, NFL
Matt Hasselbeck, NFL
Donald Glover, Actor
Cade Cunningham, NBA

OCTOBER

Pablo Picasso, Artist
Bob Night, Hall of Fame Coach
Dave Cowens, NBA
Mike Eruzione, NHL
Chad Smith, Drummer
Katy Perry, Singer

NOVEMBER

Joe DiMaggio, MLB
Joe Gibbs, NFL Coach
Ben Stein, Actor

John Larroquette, Actor
John F. Kennedy Jr., Lawyer
Jenna Bush, TV Host
Barbara Pierce Bush, Activist
Abby Phillip, CNN Host
Christina Applegate, Actress
Donovan McNabb, NFL

DECEMBER

Louis Chevrolet, Auto Racer/Cofounder Chevrolet
Humphrey Bogart, Actor
Jimmy Buffett, Singer
Barbara Mandrell, Singer
Sissy Spacek, Actress
Annie Lennox, Singer
Rickey Henderson, MLB

Chapter 8
Calendar

JANUARY

- National Blood Donor Month
- National Hobby Month
- National Hot Tea Month
- National Slavery and Human Trafficking Prevention Month
- National Soup Month

Jan 1 - New Year's Day
Jan 6 - Epiphany
Jan 20 - Martin Luther King Jr. Day
Jan 29 - Chinese New Year

FEBRUARY

- American Heart Month
- Black History Month
- National Bake for Family Fun Month
- National Hot Breakfast Month
- National Library Lover's Month
- National Snack Food Month

Feb 1 - National Freedom Day
Feb 2 - Groundhog Day

Feb 4 - Rosa Parks Day
Feb 7 - National Wear Red Day
Feb 9 - Super Bowl
Feb 12 - President Lincoln's Birthday
Feb 14 - Valentine's Day
Feb 15 - Susan B. Anthony's Birthday
Feb 17 - Presidents' Day

<u>MARCH</u>

- Irish American Heritage Month
- Multiple Sclerosis Awareness Month
- National Caffeine Awareness Month
- National Brain Injury Awareness Month
- National Nutrition Month
- Women's Awareness Month

Mar 3 - Read Across America Day
Mar 4 - Fat Tuesday/Mardi Gras
Mar 5 - Ash Wednesday
Mar 7 - Employee Appreciation Day
Mar 9 - Daylight Saving Time Starts
Mar 14 - Purim
Mar 17 - St. Patrick's Day
Mar 20 - Spring Begins
Mar 29 - Vietnam War Veterans Day

- National Month of Hope
- Distracted Driving Awareness Month
- National Child Abuse Awareness Month
- Keep America Beautiful Month
- National Autism Awareness Month
- National Parkinson Awareness Month
- National Pecan Month
- National Volunteer Month

Apr 13 - Thomas Jefferson's Birthday
Apr 13 - Passover (first day)
Apr 13 - Palm Sunday
Apr 15 - Tax Day
Apr 17 - Maundy Thursday
Apr 18 - Good Friday
Apr 18 - Arbor Day
Apr 19 - Holy Saturday
Apr 20 - Passover (last day)
Apr 20 - Easter Sunday
Apr 21 - Boston Marathon
Apr 23 - Administrative Professionals Day
Apr 24 - Take Your Child to Work Day

<u>MAY</u>

- National Dental Care Awareness Month
- National Military Appreciation Month
- National Motorcycle Awareness Month

- Date Your Mate Month
- National Barbecue Month
- National Blood Pressure Month
- National Hamburger Month

May 1 - National Day of Prayer
May 2 - Kentucky Oaks
May 3 - Kentucky Derby
May 4 - Kent State Shootings Remembrance
May 5 - Cinco de Mayo
May 6 - National Nurses Day
May 6 - Teacher Appreciation Day
May 9 - Military Spouse Appreciation Day
May 11 - Mother's Day
May 15 - Peace Officers Memorial Day
May 17 - Armed Forces Day
May 21 - Emergency Medical Services for Children Day
May 25 - National Missing Children's Day
May 25 - Friend Day
May 26 - Memorial Day
May 29 - Ascension Day

JUNE

- Aquarium Month
- Men's Health Month
- National Fresh Fruit and Vegetables Month
- National Candy Month
- National Great Outdoors Month

Jun 1-3 - Shavuot
Jun 6 - D-Day
Jun 7 - Belmont Stakes
Jun 8 - Pentecost
Jun 14 - Flag Day
Jun 14 - Army Birthday
Jun 15 - Trinity Sunday
Jun 15 - Father's Day
Jun 17 - Bunker Hill Day
Jun 19 - Juneteenth
Jun 20 - American Eagle Day
Jun 20 - Summer Begins

JULY

- National Baked Bean Month
- National Cell Phone Courtesy Month
- National Hot Dog Month
- National Ice Cream Month
- National Picnic Month

Jul 4 - Independence Day
Jul 27 - Korean War Veterans Armistice Day
Jul 27 - Parents' Day

AUGUST

- National Wellness Month
- Family Fun Month

- National Eye Exam Month
- National Golf Month
- National Sandwich Month

Aug 4 - Coast Guard Birthday
Aug 7 - Purple Heart Day
Aug 17 - National Senior Citizens Day
Aug 19 - National Aviation Day
Aug 26 - Women's Equality Day

SEPTEMBER

- Baby Safety Month
- Classical Music Month
- National Potato Month
- National Preparedness Month
- National Suicide Prevention Month

Sep 1 - Labor Day
Sep 7 - National Grandparents Day
Sep 11 - Patriot Day
Sep 17 - Constitution Day & Citizenship Day
Sep 18 - Air Force Birthday
Sep 19 - POW/MIA Recognition Day
Sep 21 - Back to Church Sunday
Sep 22 - Fall Begins
Sep 23 - Rosh Hashana
Sep 26 - Native Americans' Day

OCTOBER

- Breast Cancer Awareness Month
- Church Safety and Security Month
- Financial Planning Month
- National Book Month
- National Dessert Month
- Pastor Appreciation Month

Oct 2 - Yom Kippur
Oct 5 - Pastor Appreciation Day
Oct 6 - Child Health Day
Oct 6 - First Day of Sukkot
Oct 12 - Tabernacles Sunday
Oct 13 - Navy Birthday
Oct 13 - Columbus Day
Oct 13 - Last Day of Sukkot
Oct 15 - Simchat Torah
Oct 16 - Boss' Day
Oct 18 - Sweetest Day
Oct 31 - Halloween

NOVEMBER

- National Adoption Month
- National Diabetes Month
- National Peanut Butter Lovers Month
- NoSHAVEmber (US – Beard Month)

Nov 1 - All Saints' Day

Nov 2 - All Souls' Day
Nov 2 - Daylight Saving Time Ends
Nov 2 - New York City Marathon
Nov 4 - Election Day
Nov 10 - Marine Corps Birthday
Nov 11 - Veterans Day
Nov 23 - No Excuse Sunday
Nov 27 - Thanksgiving Day
Nov 28 - Black Friday
Nov 30 - First Sunday of Advent

DECEMBER

- AIDS Awareness Month
- National Human Rights Month
- Spiritual Literacy Month

Dec 1 - Rosa Parks Day
Dec 1 - Cyber Monday
Dec 2 - Giving Tuesday
Dec 7 - Pearl Harbor Remembrance Day
Dec 13 - National Guard Birthday
Dec 14 - Chanukah/Hanukkah Begins
Dec 21 - Winter Begins
Dec 22 - Chanukah/Hanukkah Ends
Dec 24 - Christmas Eve
Dec 25 - Christmas Day
Dec 31 - New Year's Eve

This calendar information is from www.timeanddate.com.

Chapter 9

Journaling for Jesus in 2025

I have given you 12 prophetic days in 2025 instead of 25. Write down, document, and keep a record of all the victories that God is going to give you in 2025. Pay close attention to these 12 prophetic dates for your victories. Ask God for a specific word on each of these days.

1. Saturday, January 25, 2025

____

____

____

2. Tuesday, February 25, 2025

____

____

____

3. Tuesday, March 25, 2025

____

____

____

4. Friday, April 25, 2025

____

____

____

5. Sunday, May 25, 2025

6. Wednesday, June 25, 2025

7. Friday, July 25, 2025

8. Monday, August 25, 2025

9. Thursday, September 25, 2025

____

____

____

____

10. Saturday, October 25, 2025

____

____

____

____

11. Tuesday, November 25, 2025

____

____

____

____

12. Thursday, December 25, 2025

____

____

____

____

Write out any other dates that may mean something to you:

Date   Notes

Write out any other dates that may mean something to you:

Date   Notes

Conclusion

The conclusion portion of my prophetic almanac book gives me an opportunity to put in some final thoughts that I feel God wants us to follow in that particular year. These are not just random points, or some thrown-in thoughts to end a book. They really are prophetic advice that I believe God wants us to follow. I believe with all my heart these are keys that will lead to your success in 2025 as you apply these prophetic principles to your life.

25 Prophetic Principles to Cling to in 2025

1. Life is Short, so Live in the Moment
2. Practice Forgiveness
3. Premeditate Love
4. Pay it Forward
5. Embrace What You Cannot Control
6. Speak Well of Yourself
7. Look For Solutions, Not Problems
8. Do Not Take Everything So Personal
9. Actions Speak Louder Than Words
10. Never Major on the Minors
11. Worry is Wasteful
12. Reset Your Life
13. Go the Extra Mile
14. Eliminate the Unnecessary
15. Help Those Who Are Ready to Be Helped

16.   Mind Your Own Business
17.   You Are What You Think
18.   Decisions Determine Destiny
19.   Be a Lesson or a Blessing
20.   You Cannot Fix People
21.   Set Boundaries
22.   Life is Not Fair
23.   Give Grace, Not Judgement
24.   Little Things Matter the Most
25.   God is in Charge

2025 is a year of change and with change, there must come grace. This is a Year of Grace, not just from God to us, but from us to others. Walk in these truths and establish them in your life to ensure the blessing of God upon you every single day throughout this year. A lot of things will happen that you will not understand, but you have to trust God in the middle of everything. God is still in control and will work everything out for your good. So, learn to give God grace when you do not understand the situations you face in 2025. I say it every year, but this could be the best year of your life, and that is not up to God; it is up to you. Make this year count. Make this year matter. Make this year the best year of your life.

"For I know the thoughts that I think toward you, saith the Lord, thoughts of peace, and not of evil, to give you an expected end." Jeremiah 29:11

THE END

To get daily wisdom nuggets, check out Pastor Bill on social media for the most important minute of your day!

The Minute That Matters

Scan the QR code with your phone, and you will be automatically connected to your choice of social media.

www.ingramcontent.com/pod-product-compliance
Lightning Source LLC
Chambersburg PA
CBHW071250150726
48001CB00018B/696